Skid

Pitt Poetry Series

Ed Ochester, Editor

Skid

Dean Young

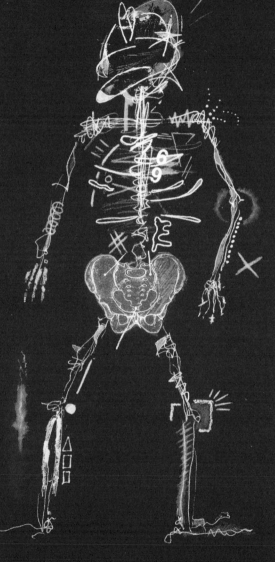

University of Pittsburgh Press

The publication of this book is supported by a grant from
the Pennsylvania Council on the Arts.

Published by the University of Pittsburgh Press,

Pittsburgh, Pa., 15260

Copyright © 2002, Dean Young

Manufactured in the United States of America

Printed on acid-free paper

10   9   8   7   6   5   4   3   2

ISBN 0-8229-5780-9

for   Robert Hass
        Roger Mitchell
        Cornelia Nixon

The main thing is not to be dead.

—Robert Motherwell

Contents

Skid

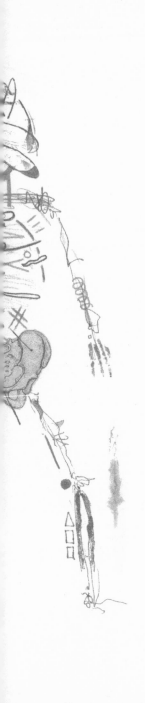

Sunflower

When Dean Young vacuums he hears
not just time's winged whatchamacallit
hurrying near but some sort of music
that isn't the motor or the attic
or the sucked-up spider's hosannas
or his mother pounded into a rectangle
or what's inside him breaking
because the only thing conclusive
all those tests showed is inside him
is some sort of crow so unsure of its
crowness, it thinks it's a stone
just as the stone thinks it's
a dark joke in the withered fields
and has to be so opaque to keep
all its ketchupy light inside because
you never know what sonuvabitch
is hanging around, waiting for a chance
to steal your thunder. When Dean Young
has his thunder, nothing moves. Not
the dust in the hose, not the music,
not even the eye of the crow. It drives him
crazy how little effect he has. He thinks
of his friends at ballparks and feels
miserable. He thinks of women's behinds
and feels radiant. He's afraid how he invented
running by moving his legs very fast
will be forgotten, attributed elsewhere.
He can't resign himself to losing the patent
on masturbation. On the other side

of the back of his head hangs his face
which he puts strawberries into.
He dreads strawberries because their mouth
is bigger than his. He dreads his wife
because he loves her. His strong opinions
re: capital punishment, arts education,
the numen dissolves in water,
the universal solvent that falls from clouds,
clouds that were HIS idea.

Bright Window

I was born through a bright window.
Winged faces, docile lions, the usual
heliocentric wires. The gods loved playing
tricks then, festooned with rags,
making the wine dregs pour forever,
switching the reels so midway through
Children of Paradise, Wile E. Coyote
creams himself again. Meep, meep,

everyone in a hurry in clouds of ink
like frightened squid. I had a friend
who spun in the rain until her makeup
melted and a scar remains on my retina.
I had a friend who thought the secret
was in turning a turntable backwards.
One pill made you stronger, one pill
and you could fly. I had a friend
who crashed us through a cornfield
and all the husks could do was sing
but that was all right, it was singing
that mattered to us, had weight,
occupied space, in motion tended
to stay in motion, at rest rest.

You start with a darkness to move through
but sometimes the darkness moves through you.

I loved those cold May mornings
stalling the wisteria,

none of the oils yet, just sketch,
the million buds of I don't know what
waiting by the stairway where no one's crying
yet, or laughing, not one leap yet in the dance,
it's almost impossible to be afraid,
the furnace kicking on one last time,
the animal dragging itself a short way
from its birth.

Sometimes I sit for hours watching people
struggle with the big glass doors,
trying to fit small lids on large cups.

You can't have it back, says the fire
affectionately. You never needed it
anyway, promises the earth.

I Am But a Traveler in This Land
& Know Little of Its Ways

Is everything a field of energy caused
by human projection? From the crib bars
hang the teething tools. Above the finger-drummed
desk, a bit lip. The cyclone fence of buts

surrounds the soccer field of what if.
Sometimes it seems like a world where no one
knows what he or she is doing, eight lanes
both directions. How about a polymer

that contracts in response to electrical
charge? A swimming pool on the 18th floor?
King Lear done by sock puppets? Anyone
who has traveled here knows the discrepancies

between idea and fact. The idea is the worm
in the tequila and the next day is the fact.
In between may be the sacred—real blood
from the wooden virgin's eyes, and the hoax—

landing sites in cornfields. Maybe ideas
are best sprung from actions like the children
of Zeus. One gives us elastic and the omelette,
another nightmares and SUVs. There's considerable

wobble in the system, and the fan belt screams,
waking the baby. Swaying in the darkened
nursery, kissing the baby-smelling head:
good idea! But also sadness looking at the sea.

The stranded whale, guided out of the cove
by tugboats, turns and swims back in.
The violinist will not let go her violin
which is 200 years old and still on the train

thus she is dragged down the track. By what
manner is the soul joined to the body?
Answer: an arm connecting a violin
to a violinist. According to Freud,

there are no accidents. Astrologists
and Presbyterians agree for different reasons.
You fall down the stairs with a birthday cake.
You try to fit a blunderbuss into a laptop.

Human consciousness: is it the projector
or the screen? They come in orange jumpsuits
and spray the grass so everything dies
but the grass. It is too late to ask Kafka

what he thinks. Sometimes they give you
a box of ash, a handshake, and the rest
is your problem. In one version,
the beggar turns out to be a king and grants

the poor couple a castle and a moat and two
silver horses said to be sired by the wind.
That was before dentistry, which might have been
a better gift. You did not want to get sick
in the 14th, 15th, 16th, 17th or 18th centuries.

So too the 19th and 20th were to be avoided
but the doctor coming to bleed you is the master
of the short story. After the kiss from whom
he will never know, the lieutenant, going home,

touches a bush in which birds are singing.

Torn Red Interior

This is the time of year people return
and can't shut up about where they've been.
Apparently the membrane's pretty baggy
stretching back to Paris. There: how easy
to go out your door and wander among the concentric
Parisianers. Here: impossible to go out your door
and wander among the concentric Parisianers. How
can anyone live in such detestable conditions?
Someone did a feasibility study once
but nothing came of it although
it still has influence in academic circles.
In Paris, people say things, things
even a rhinoceros couldn't understand
because their lips are reenacting
the coronation of Louis the $1/16^{th}$.
After the revolution, that's all
that's allowed: the upper lip's
borne in on an ermine litter
and lifted bodily by two bishops
then anointed from a purple ampulla.
The lower lip is presented with the sword of Charlemagne.
That shit don't cut it round here.
Says who? Says me, the lone star child
of Howling Lightnin All Night Long.
How do I know when the folks that raised me
inspected hams and danced like wax?
No cardinal doffing no miter
told me that's for sure but once
when I was snake-bit in a revival tent,

my aunt said, Boy, you are surely a baby of the blues.
Since then the river flowing through me
has filled with iron filings. I took a test
and they said they'd let me know but
they never let me know so now I go
on faith and gasoline, my wound
singing for its mother wound. Why,
compared to even my smallest cactus garden,
Paree is a wussy blitz of amateurs.

My People

Initially, I too appeared between the legs
of a woman in considerable discomfort.
A rather gristly scene but fairly common
among my kind. Those early days, I must
admit: a bit of a blur but generally
I was provided for, wiped off
and kept away from the well.
Dressed as a shepherdess until
I could handle an ax, it was then
I saw the golden arches and tasted of
the processed cheese and left my field
forever, disastrously it must be said
although it has led me here, addressing you
in this grand and ugly hall, paid
a nominal fee and all the grapes
I can eat. Well, I'm told they're grapes.
But I leap ahead when leaping backward
as well as vibrating in place
is more what's called for,
much like the role of the tongue
in the bell. Hear that?
Reminds me of the coyotes of our youth
before we hunted them to near extinction
then expensively reintroduced because
it turned out they were the only solution
to our rodent problem, at least
on the outside, in the cribs. Inside,
it's a grackle/possum/viper problem too,

even algae in some areas. Somehow
we've managed to ruin the sky
just by going about our business,
I in my super XL, you in your Discoverer.
A grudging and fat-cheeked tribe,
we breed without season, inadvertently
or injected with quadruplets. The gods
we played with broke, they were made of glass.
The trees our fathers planted we will not see again.

Howl Upone Eskaping, I Learne Mey Vehikle Is Not Sea-Worthie & Upone Mey Tragik Recapture & Longe Internmynt During Whyche I Wrighte These Words Thorough a Secret System Infolfing Mey Owne Blood

When I got up from my nap in 1999,
there were fewer of my kind around.
Apparently it had been circulated
that if you cracked our oblongatas
correctly, you could harvest
a fair amount of plutonium 57
although, in my experience, no one
knew the proper technique.
Still, they tried, the shattered
remains of my tribe hauled to the curb
every Monday night when the downstairs people
screamed about their ranunculi until
I called the authorities. Mid 17th century
Holland, it was tulips but now it's ranunculi.
In the bathroom was a book of poems
by H**** C*** about how sad and exquisite
and made of goopy lace everything was.
I hated those poems. Even a regular burrito,
no guacamole, was more full of life
than those poems yet each time his school
met mine, they won, walking away.
Often our guards would complain of pangs
mysterioso the night before engagement
and their hearts would go trochaic.

It was March, month of human discourse
before the human intercourse
that makes such a mess of April.
So I tried to file my report but
part of what I wanted I knew I'd never get
yet when I didn't, I felt driven to account
for the contrary forces within.
Can you see what I was up against?
I was just like you until I was alone
then I was a cherry blossom.

Gaga Gala

At the Institute of Haiku-Induced
Orgasm, the reading was nearly over
before it began. In Iowa City, when
my friend read his poem about styling
his dead mother's wig, it was like
he was the only member of our tribe
with a heart that still worked. I wonder,
Does anyone hear the Hare Krishnas
outside passing near? At the Center
for Useless Experimentation, my poem
about sick swans went over big although
no one caught that it was really about
Keats's tuberculosis.
After five minutes in the Writers' Gaggle
to benefit a citywide neutering
by the ASPCA, the woman who read
about her genitals handcuffed
to the Washington Monument
asked if I could believe there was nothing
to drink. Nope, but everyone knows
at least one story of Dylan Thomas
hitting the orchestra pit and Dionysus
throwing up all over his blue tunic.
The lamb on his shoulder doesn't
have a head. Dirty dirty dirty, intones
Cotton Mather into the microphone.
Sylvia Plath: head of a Roman emperor,
lips of Tinker Bell. The lamb on her shoulder
doesn't have a head. Antonin Artaud,

not someone you'd expect in charge
but here he is, in charge:
zzzzpktzzzzzzzzzzzpktzzzpktpkttt
as if the forces of the cosmos are still
threshing out the human soul.
Chainsaw rackmold tungsten noose. Okay,
I'm convinced but something still seems missing.
The white answer never fits the white
question. In New York, at the Council
for Public Poetry Safety, the great-eared,
glassy-winged elder says he remembers me
from Arizona although I've never been to Arizona.
Ah, Arizona, I try to convey into his bushy eyeholes,
buggy narcotic vulvaular windswept idyllic screwed-up Arizona,
since then I've not been the same.
The winter morning is a stone
written upon by evaporation.
The summer evening a sheet
on which a thousand poets try to sleep.
One reads for an hour about
the brain surgery of her horse,
another weeps, cluing in the audience,
and a coat falls away from the other coats
as if with great effort. In the case of helium,
first they knew it was there then
they found it. With the electron,
first they found it then
it proved not to be there.

Blue Garden

A dog tied to a parking meter
should never give up theorizing
the curve in the continuum where space
becomes time and time becomes a big
bowl of grub. A poem should be able
to say that in one word but maybe that word
is zypxtflo. A poem should be a window
and breaking the window behind which
the mannequins are made of springs,
headless, pendulous, full of sex
just as gladiolas are full of sex
and the ferry terminal. A poem should be
a noise then it should know when to shut up.
It should be naked in the rain or nearly so.
A poem should be all gussied up for the funeral.
There should be dirt tanging the air
and pings as shovels hit the dirt.
It shouldn't be afraid of the repetitious dirt.
Within reason: personal anecdote.
As the rain wetted her dress,
he thought about Balboa
which was one of the ways we knew
something was odd with him.
A poem should be odd as a small cast-iron platypus.
In the cafés, all the scribblers should stop
upon the word THE not because there's nothing
or too much to follow
but that the the the that the the
seems like a turning note of such importance

to the roundelay, whatever's next can't possibly
be so drenched in revelation.
Then again.
A poem should resist the intelligence and Wallace Stevens
almost successfully. Never put an éclair in a suitcase
or a poem. Friends may be included the way air
is included in a bouncing ball.
Suffering, naturally,
but no one should die. Make that almost no one.
A poem should not be talking.
Gliff through sometimely canoe.
In a poem called "Blue Garden,"
forget about the blue, the garden
as indication of the unavoidability of loss
and failure. Ouch. Sadness tastes like aluminum,
joy like crystallized ginger.
Zypxtflo. Zypxtflo.
The truest endings are abrupt.

Side Effects

Your papillae momentus is shot, these pills
may help but you'll probably lose your right arm.
My right arm! How will I live? So the client
thrashes out of the office like a man learning
to swim by drowning but after a couple weeks
he can almost float, button his own coat.
So he goes back to the specialist who says,
I bet your Palace of Moranzini's collapsed,
maybe this drug will work, it seems to have
some effect on black widow bites, only thing is
you'll have to lose your lake. My lake!
For days afterward, everyone he sees is carrying
a kayak, nautical analogies overflow
even the financial section. Now would be
a good time for a couple strangelets to shred
the fabric of reality but his experiments
at the cyclotron don't amount to much dark matter
so reality goes on with a sloshing sound,
a pointless flopping in his chest then the doctor
says, It's got to be your heart and the man cries out,
Lord, you've got me in your tweezers now!
Ha, ha, what an opportunity to meet the deductible,
you just fly three inches over yourself
and declare a national disaster. Look
at those miserable robots down there
trying to start their cars, pay their interest,
cook eggplant. Let's see what happens
when we drop this big rock, saith the Lord,
the whole planet wobbling on its loose axle
while the patients come and go, some getting weaker,
buying expensive sunglasses and losing them,

some getting stronger, buying expensive sunglasses
and breaking them, puddled in mud, the bones
ground down and thrown upon the hibiscus
to encourage sturdier blooms.
So the waters freeze and melt, the mountains
rise and shrug, the bolts of the Ferris wheel
loosen and are tightened, snow approaches
the house and turns back, forgetting why it came.
So the dead father says in the dream, I didn't
want you to know but now you know. BAM BAM BAM,
you think you want out but you want in.
You're on the wrong side of the door.
You're on the fifth green when the lightning comes.
You're halfway through your sandwich
and they've already taken your plate.
The food is good here but the service
crazy and you wonder why you came,
why you've been coming for years and still
no one knows you. Because no one knows you?
Silly you to be known anyway
now that the grid is showing,
the chicken wire they affix the flowers to.
It's almost 3 and the rain has stopped.
The sun comes out and it's not an accusation
or a plea. You can sit in it for a minute.
Drink your tea before the declensions
of evening into the infinitive of sleep.
First you will wake in disbelief, then
in sadness and grief and when you wake
the last time, the forest you've been
looking for will turn out to be
right in the middle of your chest.

Dead Dean

I'm thinking about the dead Dean
swimming in the night's muscle.
It's good to see him up and about,
recovered from who knows what
who knows how, enjoying the cherry
on top of the purgative, the weather
with its fists of tulips and nails.

I love to watch him come out of the rain
struggling with his octopi, getting the singe
back in his eye. Him and his corollaries,
him and his postulates. Don't even
get him started on the genitalia
of atoms. Don't be fooled by clarity,
there's always something behind it.

Sometimes he likes to gather us novices
under a rain shelter, smoke rising
from his shoulders the way it does
from the edges of equations where
the blade's stropped so thin it disappears.
Nothing can cut him then. Not the hornets
in his message box, not the curriculum.
About there being no dancers among
the dead, Lorca was wrong. The dead Dean
shoots out a pseudopod and it's dancing.
The dead Dean nods off—dancing! He walks

a strange city, streetlights disconnected
laughter, square coins. Fierce and fiercer
the road rose, the word rose. He creates
an air of secrecy to support the myth
of intimacy which is often accomplished
by opacity. Not bad for a guy who bleeds
so fast, half his sandwich is blood.
Hey na yeah yah go go uh oh dead Dean!

Sources of the Delaware

I love you he said but saying it took twenty years
so it was like listening to mountains grow.
I love you she says fifty times into a balloon
then releases the balloon into a room
whose volume she calculated to fit
the breath it would take to read
the complete works of Charlotte Brontë aloud.
Someone else pours green dust into the entryway
and puts rice paper on the floor. The door
is painted black. On the clothesline
shirttails snap above the berserk daffodils.
Hoagland says you've got to plunge the sword
into the charging bull. You've got
to sew yourself into a suit of light.
For the vacuum tube, it's easy,
just heat the metal to incandescence
and all that dark energy becomes a radiance.
A kind of hatching, syntactic and full of buzz.
No contraindications, no laws forbidding
buying gin on Sundays. No if you're pregnant,
if you're operating heavy machinery because
who isn't towing the scuttled tonnage
of some self? Sometimes just rubbing
her feet is enough. Just putting out
a new cake of soap. Sure, the contents
are under pressure and everyone knows
that last step was never intended to bear
any weight but isn't that why we're standing there?
Ripples in her hair, I love you she hollers

over the propellers. Yellow scarf in mist.
When I planted all those daffodils,
I didn't know I was planting them
in my own chest. Play irretrievably
with the lid closed, Satie wrote on the score.
But Hoagland says he's sick of opening
the door each morning not on diamonds
but piles of coal, and he's sick of being
responsible for the eons of pressure needed
and the sea is sick of being responsible
for the rain, and the river is sick of the sea.
So the people who need the river
to float waste to New Jersey
throw in antidepressants. So the river
is still sick but nervous now too,
its legs keep thrashing out involuntarily,
flooding going concerns, keeping the president
awake. So the people throw in beta-blockers
to make it sleep which it does, sort of,
dreaming it's a snake again but this time
with fifty heads belching ammonia
which is nothing like the dreams it once had
of children splashing in the blue of its eyes.
So the president gets on the airways
with positive vectors and vows
to give every child a computer
but all this time, behind the podium,
his penis is shouting, Put me in, Coach,
I can be the river! So I love you say
the flashbulbs but then the captions
say something else. I love you says

the hammer to the nail. I love Tamescha
someone sprays across the For Sale sign.
So I tell Hoagland it's a fucked-up ruined
world in such palatial detail, he's stuck
for hours on the phone. Look at those crows,
they think they're in on the joke and
they don't love a thing. They think
they have to be that black to keep
all their radiance inside. I love you
the man says as his mother dies
so now nothing ties him to the earth,
not fistfuls of dirt, not the silly songs
he remembers singing as a child.
I love you I say meaning lend me twenty bucks.

Today's Visibility

I don't know what I was thinking
taking us to the Museum of Surgery
but we left very glad of anesthetic
and the sky entirely not cut open.

Later, it was nearly impossible to see
the haystacks because it turned out
we were in the Museum of Museum Guards.
One woman was eight feet tall, her head

a spectacular aluminum oval that floated
around the gallery. But the exhibit
of Incan placemats turned out to be
an exhibit of descriptions of Incan

placemats because the mats themselves
were too delicate to be looked at.
Certainly the Museum of Shadows
was full of shadows but I got the feeling

people were seeing things I wasn't.
A window made you cry in a good way.
I wanted to go to the Museum of Staircases
because of what happened once in Rome

but by the time we found the escalator
to catch the elevator, we realized
the Retrospect of the Future
would soon be closed so we rushed away.

The Museum of Weather was between shows
(again) and you felt tetchy and volumetric
so we went to the Café of One Thousand
Adjectives where they searched for a sandwich.

Afterwards, the driver of our museum-quality
cab was from the Ivory Coast and seemed
to want to take us there. I loved what
was happening to your hair in the Museum

of This Moment we did share. A man ran
between the blocked cars trying to sell
a rose, chunks of ice bobbing in the lake.

We Through Mists Descry

So much energy. People buying watermelons,
boarding airplanes, watching their parents die
and writing poems about it while above throbs
the celestial. I love how sadness turns
celebratory, the childlike apocalyptic.
Bees return to their hives, freighted
with nectars. Shadows rise from the mud,
flinging back their wet hair and even though
this seashell is very small, it's still singing
about the void. Often great tension arises
between sincerity and rhetoricity imposing
vague profundities. Outside a man is failing
to push-start his car, albeit a very polished car.
Remember how rash Apollo was even while inventing
trigonometry? He did it to impress some skinny kid
milking a goat, after all. Let's not forget
the head in the furnace, how burning is
laughing and laughing is also crying out.
When my father died, I saw his spirit snagged
in a tree, a woman running across the parking lot,
windows full of smoke. When my father died,
his spirit snagged in a tree then left behind
its last body of plastic bags. I saw the sky
wring its blue until it cracked and oils
leaked out. I thought I was seeing everything
and could turn off the white light with a switch.
Satellite dishes in every yard, shiny, shiny stars.
I'd like to be completely free but I want everything
to belong to me. You fall upon the thorns of life
and bleed and people think you're a fool. But later,

at the cash bar, the disputants are transformed
by the lips of their eyes, the sex organs
of exhaled cigarette smoke. Even if it's only
skin-deep, once you derive the area, consider
how the skin goes into the ears, behind the eyes,
down the throat, that's an awful lot of beauty.
Once someone told me I should live by water.
Once someone sold me a surge protector for every room.

Snowy Prairie Rabbit

Mary Ruefle was born in Missouri
parenthetical to all entreaty.
Through no fault of her own,
she has traveled widely
from aspergillum swap meet to swap meet,
teaching at Vermont College, Bellingham University
and currently in some Ohio state.
Even a brief study
shows the snowy rabbit's life
far more regimented than we would ever suppose.
Rue: an aromatic plant yielding a volatile
oil formally used medicinally.
During her baby tornado years
when most people can't get out of the way of their own capes,
Mary invented lassitudinous head-wounds
that still influence hat-making abroad.
In the event of a water landing, your seat
becomes a flotation device—that was Mary's
idea. Ditto the preheat function.
Rue: to feel remorse or sorrow, to regret
and repent. When the Gauls came upon us
in the '70s, after a disgraceful resistance
marked by gratuitous sleeping pills
devoid of actual sleeping, it was Mary who,
watching from her tub of milk,
penned the anthems we most wish to sing
but never do that nonetheless synchronize
all our duskier cries. When I first met Mary,
she was having serious barbecuing problems.
All the corpuscles were breaking

and you know those things you sometime see
in the road: apparitions of floating lakes,
mirages of big rocks, beady-eyed hallucinations?
Well, I'd been driving right over them for years
doing what to myself I dare not ask.
But enough of me. Once there was a little girl
who couldn't stop hopping and squinching up
her nose so they sent her to a doctor
who prescribed injections for the little girl
who couldn't stop pretending she was a rabbit
because otherwise she'd become a rabbit,
the annals are full of such cases,
and think how sad her family would be
feeding her only turnip greens,
keeping her outside even in winter,
how the dog, even in friendliness,
might rip her legs off.
We are very lucky tonight.

Bright Head

Unspeakable things have happened to you
but so too speakable. You've soaked up
a lot. When I painted the door blue,
you came through. As one gets older,
there's more and more of you in the past,
mostly unnoticed at the time like
a foot that does not hurt. A man
walks into a bar. In 1976,
you were a mimosa outside my window
I could climb to get in my window.
Damn you, I don't know what you are
so you become a foreign language, traffic,
goo. A spider climbs out of my shoe.
The voice cries out. Only the moon
answers. The winged males fall to earth
and are eaten by trout. Darling, I
am tired and worn. My shirt is torn
where twice it has been sewn. Sometimes
I love you most when you are filled
with little seeds. You grow opaque
when heated, something happening
to your proteins. I've seen you ruined
by spring drizzle but survive suicides.
The Irish think they own you but you sleep
beside me like a bride. I have tried
to refrain from freakish movements,
a long spike sticking out my chest
like a highly ineffective way of attracting
a mate. I have tried to keep my answers

under sixty seconds, my dead father
in his hundredth mask spare-changing
outside Radio Shack. A giraffe's heart
is two feet long. A slow roux is a due roux.
Bright head, weird heart. Knock knock.
When you are the Golden Gate, your toll's
$3 going south. When you are a lion,
we can find you by sending beaters
into the bush but you are most yourself
when you find us. Excuse me, is that your
car alarm? Translation: please take off
your clothes. In 1968, you were given to me
in the form of a rubber snake by my uncle
with a string of firecrackers.
The last time I saw him, he couldn't
work the 3,000 muscles it takes to say
Get me out of here. It was cake time.
I had been sorely afraid but Go ahead,
you said, jump. The chute opens.

This Living Hand

It's not only the word roses
lurking inside neurosis or the fact
that most of my formal education
occurred in the midwest, so too
my summer job inhaling industrial
reactants should be considered.
It's an unstable world, babe.
Always an inner avalanche
as they say in receiving.
I'm sure if I'd gotten a shot
of Karl instead of Zeppo Marx
in utero, things would have turned out
differently. Instead, my mother
went right on eating lobster.
But where were we? Weren't you
over there struggling with your territory?
How did that go? Do you feel your coworkers
were supportive? Did anyone lay hands
upon you? Dreams are down the hall.
If you were shot into outer space
and came back in a hundred years, unaged,
what would you find? What can you do
personally to ensure that never happens?
Will you have my baby? It's amazing
anything ever gets done around here.
Everyone thinks even changing vase water
is in someone else's purview as if
this is a place where rivers flow backwards
and children balance eggs on end

demonstrating forces at work, ordinary
forces come to deranged circumstances.
I'm not exactly one of those ruined folk
with a narrative tied round my neck but
I have obviously seen too many movies
in which people transform into wolves,
reptiles, metal reptiles, poisonous clouds,
vegetarians, bunny-boilers, organs
of the other side, strippers stripping
to fund the needs of a special child,
to be of use regarding: work load,
love forlornness, travel arrangements
(don't go but if you do, don't come back),
moose behavior (I have heard however
they should not be approached),
chandelier installation that does or
does not require rewiring. Ditto
checkbook balancing, rifle-repair
of current manufacture or flintlock,
all forms of testifying, arbitration,
and/or surgery although in an emergency,
say if a bee flew in your mouth and
stung your windpipe thereby swelling
closed your throat, I could perhaps
be prevailed upon to attempt a tracheotomy
with this very pen
with which I write these words.

Chest Pains of the Romantic Poets

If the spirit is to entangle the commonplace
in the congeries of the impossible,
I missed my chance with the tall Dutch girls.
I wasn't 23, wasn't in Amsterdam where I
couldn't muster a sensible consonant cluster
through a cytoplasmic hash cloud when they didn't
materialize like frost, like details illuminated
by overwrought monks. I couldn't walk but I could
dance, and they weren't shining discs when they didn't
take me home and kick off their acid-washed jeans
and their breasts weren't lamps on the decks of fogged-in
ships, their thighs weren't scrawled with a silver
script I would kneel to read, their sex wasn't
delicate voracious sea life and their eyes . . .
I can't say a thing about their eyes.
Outside, even the shadows froze but I didn't
stay a week watching their six-inch TV
when they went off and did I don't know what,
not eating whatever they gave me, chocolate, beer,
something that once was fish, losing almost
five pounds. I can't remember how one wrinkled
her brow when she swallowed, the way the other
sighed, my friends not wondering if I was alive
until one afternoon, I didn't leave,
never seeing them again.

Whale Watch

Sometimes you may feel alone and crushed
by what you cannot accomplish
but the thought of failure is a fuzz
we cannot rid ourselves of
anymore than the clouds can their moisture.
Why would they want to anyway?
It is their identity and purpose
above the radish and radicchio fields.
Just because a thing can never be finished
doesn't mean it can't be done.
The most vibrant forms are emergent forms.
In winter, walk across the frozen lake
and listen to it boom and you will know
something of what I mean.
It may be necessary to go to Mexico.
Do not steal tombstones but if you do,
do not return them as this is sentimental
and the sentimental is a larval feeling
that bloats and bloats but never pupates.
Learn what you can of the coyote and shark.
Do not encourage small children
to play the trombone as the shortness
of their arms may prove quite frustrating,
imprinting a lifelong aversion to music
although in rare cases a sense of unreachability
may inspire operas of delicate auras.
If you hook, try to slice.
I have not the time to fully address
Spinoza but put Spinoza on your list.

Do not eat algae.
When someone across the table has a grain of rice
affixed to his nostril, instead of shouting,
Hey, you got rice hanging off your face!
thereby perturbing the mood
as he speaks of his mother one day in the basement,
brush your nose as he watches
and hidden receptors in the brain
will cause him to brush his own nose
ergo freeing the stupid-looking-making rice.
There is so much to say and shut up about.
As regards the ever-present advice-dispensing susurration
of the dead, ignore it; they think everyone's
going to die. I have seen books with pink slips
marking vital passages
but this I do not recommend
as it makes the book appear foolish
like a dog in a sweater.
Do not confuse size with scale:
the cathedral may be very small,
the eyelash monumental.
Know yourself to be made mostly of water
with a trace of aluminum, a metal
commonly used in fuselages.
For flying, hollow bones are best or
no bones at all as in the honeybee.
Do not kill yourself.
Do not put the hammer in the crystal carafe
except as a performance piece.
When you are ready to marry,
you will know but if you don't,

don't worry. The bullfrog never marries,
ditto the space shuttle
yet each is able to deliver its payload:
i.e. baby bullfrogs and satellites, respectively.
When young, fall in and out of love like a window
that is open and only about a foot off the ground.
Occasionally land in lilacs
or roses if you must
but remember, the roses
have been landed in many times.
If you do not surprise yourself,
you won't surprise anyone else.
When the yo-yo "sleeps," give a little tug
and it will return unless it has "slept" too long.
Haiku should not be stored with sestinas
just as one should never randomly mix
the liquids and powders beneath the kitchen sink.
Sand is both the problem and the solution for the beach.
To impress his teacher, Pan-Shan lopped off
his own hand, but to the western mind,
this seems rather extreme.
Neatly typed, on-time themes
strongly spelled are generally enough.
Some suggest concentrating on one thing
for a whole life but narrowing down
seems less alluring than opening up
except in the case of the blue pencil
with which to make lines on one side
of the triangle so it appears to speed through the firmament.
Still, someone should read everything
Galsworthy wrote. Everyone knows
it's a race but no one's sure of the finish line.

You may want to fall to your knees
and beg forgiveness without knowing precisely
for what. You may have a hole in your heart.
You may solve the equation but behind it
lurks another equation. You may never get
what you want and feel like you're already a ghost
and a failed ghost at that, unable to walk through walls.
There will be a purple hat. Ice cream.
You may almost ruin the wedding.
You may try to hang yourself but be saved
by a kid come home early from school
or you may be that kid who'll always remember
his mother that day in the basement,
how she seemed to know he'd done something wrong
before he even knew
and already forgave him,
the way she hugged him and cried.
Nothing escapes damage for long,
not the mountain or the sky.
You may be unable to say why
a certain song makes you cry until
it joins the other songs,
even the one that's always going on
and is never heard, the one that sings us into being.
On the phone, the doctor may tell you to come in.
It may rain for three days straight.
Already you've been forgiven,
given permission. Each week, cryptograms
come with the funny papers.
You're not alone.
You may see a whale.

Shamanism 101

Like everyone, I wanted my animal
to be the hawk.

I thought I wanted the strength
to eat the eyes first then tear
into the fuse box of the chest
and soar away.

I needed help because I still
cowered under the shadow of my father,
a man who inspected picture tubes
five out of seven nights,

who woke to breakfast on burnt roast
except the two weeks he'd sleep
on a Jersey beach and throw me
into the gasoline-sheened waves.
I loved him dying indebted
not knowing to what,

thinking his pension would be enough,
released not knowing from what,
gumming at something I was afraid
to get close enough to hear, afraid
of what I was co-signing. So maybe

the elephant. The elephant knows
when one of its own is suffering
up to six miles away. Charges across
the desert cognizant of the futility.
How can I be forgiven when I don't know
what I need forgiving for? Sometimes

the urges are too extreme: to slap
on the brakes and scream, to bite the haunch
of some passing perfume, so maybe my animal
is the tiger. Or shark.

Or centipede.

But I know I'm smaller than that,
filling notebooks with clumsy versions
of one plaint, one pheromonal call,

clamoring over a crumb that I think
is the world, baffled by the splotch
of one of my own crushed kind,
almost sweet, a sort of tar,
following a trail of one or two molecules,

leaving a trail
of one or two molecules.

Honeycomb

One wakes up glad
that the errands of sleep
are over.
The day is yours
to fritter away on consciousness,
goldfinches
hammering foil over foil,
the sunglasses missing a wing
drawn from the glove box
in sudden sun.
So what will your allotment
of joy and terror be?
A blood test?
The usual business at the rink?
All along the hollow body
drill holes
an inch and a half apart
and you've got yourself a flute.
Fire penetrates the brainpan
like syrup, sweet glue,
its blush turns out to be
pigment ground from bricks.
Such is the constitution of matter
in these dimensions—
it's always something,
some gorilla in the parking lot
or the boys in research
cooking up a new spill.
But what fun to walk

the resilient walkways
over the roof of Dis,
just here and there
from the sewer lids'
nipples,
bursts of steam.
This is the place
where I was a student.
See, here are students now
memorizing the parts of the bee.
And here's where I first
tried to speak
to my only love,
on this bridge
over a sheet of ice.
It was only later,
at Ye Olde Wash House,
that the process seemed
so unlikely and ordained
by the random plunking
of particle into particle
which in one case
levels mountains,
another produces light.

Lives of the Mind

I wake in pjs crenellated and badged,
my head full of 18th century French
battle strategies. My god! I'm Napoleon!
What can I possibly say to my creative
writing class now? How stop Heather
from deliquescing when I explain why
Ed thought her poem about her grandfather's
funeral was about a fashion show?
Heather, good specifics but

you must attack in a pincer with the foot
then follow on the flank with the horse.
You must try to appear bigger than you are
when encountering the coyote. You must
move towards the body blow even though
it's counterintuitive, then when
the baby's out, dry it off and keep it warm.
No need to cut the cord unless

the hospital's miles away.
All the wrong people are dreaming of Duchamp.
Art is one prolonged un-understanding
just as dawn is day's un-understanding of night
and while suffering may not ennoble,
it sure sweetens the singing voice. Oh,
how I miss those small flaky cakes
of Corsica. Frequent urination
is often a problem for older men

but no one's having the problems I'm having.
Retreat? Never! I believe this heart
will be my only heart, this mule my only mule.
A shadow races through me, profaning
the sky, and I walk without a companion wolf.
Ridges of high pressure, continued valley
heat, these wounds are not deep
but go the whole way through.

Flight Pattern

Across the street, rope hangs
from an excited cherry tree, a chair
knocked over beneath. You can tell
what a good neighborhood this is
by how quickly they cut down the suicides
(see fig. 1). Dissecting children to ascertain
concentrations of heavy metals in the liver
also provides helpful information (see fig. 2)
but one must work through complex tunnels
to initiate such a study and I don't know
about you, but that sort of hooey makes me blue.
I'd just as soon search people's trash
under the cover of darkness
which is not to be confused
with the cover of brightness
oft employed by the gods
as they'd ogle us bathing and milking our goats
oh oh oh oh oh oh oh oh oh oh oh
(please tear along perforations)
then try to turn us into parakeets.
But as far as those gods go,
they turned out to be quite easy
to dispose of although you can still find a few
in pawn shops trying to grope the Breasts
of the Infinite, chipped and worse for wear
amongst the forlorn Stratocasters and pitching wedges.
Forlorn! The very word is like a bell
to call me back to myself
but let's check with Dean at the Storm Desk.
Dean? Well, Dean, as you can see from the radar,

there's a hairy super cell fronting a real dick
of low pressure, repressing the unstable
air mass which is life and as these isobars
make clear, now is no time to be setting out
onion starts let alone assuming a landing pattern
over Detroit, the Motor City. Thanks, Dean,
but don't bother trying to help these people,
they are a becalmed and callous lot,
full of toxic moxy, fattened on the comprehensible.
What do they know of our suffering?
What do they know of holding a blossom
in your palm and whispering it your weakest
secrets and all the petals falling off?

Goodbye, Place I Lived Nearly 23 Years Almost Everyone Left Before Me

How full you got of people to hate
with only a couple stranded poets.
Poor Anthony. Poor Laura. Where
is the duende? Not in Oddbody Hall
full of identity and choke weed.
Identity is always whining and someone's
always to blame. What a rotten place
for even a single copy of *Lunch Poems*.
It was sad to see one last time the ash
I planted over my cat, Mescalito
behind the rooms on West 6th where
my girlfriend hated me, no, loved me,
no, will it ever end? It ended.
July 4th, alone, making macaroni salad
for 20 and Fleeson called. Someone stole
his dueling pistols, he wanted me
to get word out to his 6,000,000 recent
whirlygigged exes that they were entirely
ornamental and if someone tried to shoot
for instance him, the gun would probably
explode. For $\frac{1}{2}$ a semester I understood
the kidney. Goodbye, Nicks Pub no apostrophe
where I agreed with Kevin about James Wright
even after finding the Desnos poem
"Lying in a Hammock" is filched from.
My surrealism had thus far only infected
my personal life. There was no other life.
When I told Scott my father died,

he told me he was gay. A trade? Yes
but no. I did LSD, lay in bed and tried
to astral project until I had to pee.
Tragically, I took over Sue's damaged iguana.
When I dove from the quarry ledge no one would,
everyone did.

Hammer

Every Wednesday when I went to the shared office
before the class on the comma, etc.,
there was on the desk, among
the notes from students aggrieved and belly-up
and memos about lack of funding
and the quixotic feasibility memos
and labyrinthine parking memos
and quizzes pecked by red ink
and once orange peels,
a claw hammer.
There when I came and there when I left,
it didn't seem in anyone's employ.
There was no room left to hang anything.
It already knew how to structure an argument.
It already knew that it was all an illusion
that everything hadn't blown apart
because of its proximity to oblivion,
having so recently come from oblivion itself.
Its epiphyses were already closed.
It wasn't my future that was about to break its wrist
or my past that was god knows where.
It looked used a number of times
not entirely appropriately
but its wing was clearly healed.
Down the hall was someone with a glove
instead of a right hand.
A student came by looking for who?
Hard to understand
then hard to do.
I didn't think much of stealing it,

having so many hammers at home.
There when I came, there when I left.
Ball peen, roofing, framing, sledge, one
so small of probably only ornamental use.
That was one of my gifts,
finding hammers by sides of roads, in snow, inheriting,
one given by a stranger for a jump in the rain.
It cannot be refused, the hammer.
You take the handle, test its balance
then lift it over your head.

Changing Your Bulb

I disconnect the power for at least
five minutes until your bulb is cool
and no longer producing song through
small chewing devices at the end
of its beak. Clunk goes the tipped-over
pounce-meat. When I change your bulb,
am I really changing my own? This concludes
these opening remarks. Later you will be asked
to repeat them as a test of metal decay.
Now take your steel ring by any sharp
of tool at place of two gap or at least
that's what the instructions say.
Maybe you were made in Tunisia.
I have loved you longer than my one life.
In the North, Siegfried rests after his hunt.
The new adults go into summer hibernation,
called aestivation but we are just waking.
Wing-wear: always a troublement, but there,
in the Wild Valley and Forest of the Rhine,
your new bulb gets installed, acting mainly
as an exacerbation to fuzzy brain function.
I feel like I'm approaching a cliff wrapped
in an enormous kite, cheery as life insurance
and I can't be sure if the statuary
is of rich citizens or supernatural forces.
Finite is our sadness upon this earth she-bop.
Smoke is the voice uh-huh, hammer the moment
sha-la, one magic sleep ends beginning another.
So I insert your glass shield back into your reflector

and it is like you have never been gone.
In the distance, Valhalla is burning
and the old gods calmly await their pupation
in unprotected crevices. There is a part
of the spirit that can not be destroyed.

Republican Victory

In the field, the complex snowmen
have been kicked apart. Some had used
the familiar scarecrow matrix,
others were dead inside, cloned
like modern clocks.

Someone has squeezed the tube out.
Someone has broken the lever off.

I bet this deflated football was a pancreas.
Was it a question of oxygen to the brain?
Here's a whole family: sad.

Soon this field will be hash-marked again,
tackling dummies in formation.
My hands are cold.

At some point, I gave up my youthful
dream of robotics, of handling toxic substances
with remote control arms. Soon
there will be robots small enough
to enter the bloodstream but probably
too late for you and me.

Have you ever looked down
upon your laid-open self and felt
only mildly abashed, foreshortened,
unsequestered, wind in your ears?

That's when the people of the future
contact me with a song
that's actually a series of beeps because
that's what music has become for them,
the people of the future.

Some of their faces are sewn together wrong
so it looks like their pigtails are too tight.

I wish they could tell us all we've done
hasn't come to naught although to them
naught might not be all that bad,
no acid rain, no gappers' block,
where even the homeless can find a home
or at least in theory.

But these thoughts, I'm told,
are but junk mail in a maelstrom
to the people of the future.

They wear shiny visors.
They have beer that glows.
They have rivers that glow.
They'll never forgive us.

The River Merchant, Stuck in Kalamazoo, Writes His Wife a Letter during Her Semester Abroad

We were looking forward to being alive.
Now you new place! Me not too! Strange taste
afternoon lonely for hummingbird mouthful.
You somewhere else make everywhere else
elser. I know almost nothing about this flower
growing from my chest. Does it need deadheading?
Only you not answer. This complete the test
of the emergency broadcast system? Definition
of the female breasts as modified sweat gland
certainly leave out curfew-breaking! Sunny melon
morning all day! Remember! In my dream, almost
get your sash off then wake of sadness. Forceful
but gentle I not girl-scaring want to explain
not like Jim explain his night in jail so
fly-around he explain other nights in jail.
No hello river in the sky then. When someone
love you, good to be afraid-making in that way? Not
nice among dumb bamboo thickets, gazillion
crickets not one Thelonius Monk. Ha ha
only so long. I grow cold. Soon snow
fall on the no more factory.

Roller Coaster

The leg braces on the stuffed bunny
didn't help it hop but they sure
scared people. The blizzard was not
a bit tired crouching over the flint.
The man who invented the roller coaster
wasn't angry but he couldn't bring
anyone back from the dead especially
himself. The six arms just wouldn't fit
into one jacket. Everything crashes to earth
said Yvette, roe link uppers tock tock tock—
he adjusted the shutter speed—
rolling up her stocking. How did God
manage to hide eternity in such obvious
places? A grape, a girder, the spoon
in the back of the knee. Copper wire
wound into a motor. Try pulling yourself
through a silk knot of yourself *voila*
and you'll see. Go ahead, try.
What's brighter than magnesium ignited?
Like the fox, he started with questions.
How did you get here? Are you hurt?
How many fingers am I holding up?
How big was the paw print?
How do you recognize your love?
How can you be sure it wasn't a trick?
Didn't you smell the acetate?
How were you found? You were in the area,
weren't you? What did it look like
hovering there?

Saga of Stumps

When Vasistha threw himself from the firmament
in anguish, his fall was broken by layer
after layer of lotus flowers
because halfway through the story
it became obvious the sun was too big
and had to be whittled down
and that's where all the gods and peoples came from,
radiant shavings and curlicues, scalding chips and dust
and that's why everyone feels like residue,
hacked-off and blistered, squirting
across the ionosphere.

So that's the first anguish
of which all the other anguishes are sparks
landing on sofas, in hair, carried by breezes
to the shake roofs so every now and then
the hills of Berkeley can return to the first element
from which all comes and in which all is destroyed
except the salamander.

But because Vasistha was a god, his anguish
could not be extinguished. Even after he cut off
his own head with his thumbnail,
it just went on wailing in complex metrics
and occasionally out of the mouth
new beings would sprout: the flamingo like a bouquet
pulled from a bucket of glue, Gerard Manley Hopkins,
the mountain bike, the running shoe

and then one afternoon, my friend vomits the thirty
sleeping pills and they swim along the floor like polliwogs
so he knows which god is his father and like his father
his headless body must stumble through the stinging smoke,
grope through storms of butterflies, tearing
the finery of courtesans and when he laughs
there is no sound and when he cries just a far-off
desert wind like the susurration of students
down the hall solving equations.

So at first he sticks a candle in his neck
but the wax keeps dripping in his soup
so then he stuffs in the wadded drafts
of his epic suicide note which at least stops
the bleeding and makes his colleagues ask him
to serve on the department council because
he seems so conscientious what with a head
of crumpled paper but then one day he hears

about a group with sewing machines for heads
and they get together once a week to stitch
the vast tapestry that is this story and when
they are thus employed it sounds like flocks
of tiny birds swirling from bush to bush
sometimes in fright, sometimes to feed
on lightning bugs and sometimes it sounds
like everything burning, and he thinks,
Let everything burn, so for a while his anguish
is part of the design, red thread running
through the sea like a sciatic nerve
and this is how things go for a million years

until one day in the bathroom, he finds his face
floating in the sink and splashes it back on.
It feels at first like a jellyfish and looks
like it was used as a mop but when he rejoins
his friends, the one whose hands were beetles
in a previous life, the one who is only at home
in the mountains, sister with a dead parent
attached by elastic, brother poisoned by his cure,
the blunt scissors, the boiling water, the one
he's slept with off and on since the wreck
of his marriage says, Hey, don't I know you,
grass growing from her mouth.

All the King's Men

Already February and he hasn't even nailed
a single boxing glove to the wall. Because
he kept putting his head inside white rock
he missed his appointment with clouds
so the clouds wrote dismissive reviews.
The reason you never see black birds
at symphonies is orchestral music
makes them explode. Because everything
is cash and carry, he crossed out slogans
so you'd read them, slept in castles
and cardboard boxes simultaneously.
The last thing that came out of Basquiat
was a beautiful pink foam. Not a crown
or a copyright, not a skeleton
~~riding a skeleton horse.~~
Was he trying to disprove his body
was a ~~dream~~ forgery? He broke off
his father's esophagus but it grew back.
On Tuesdays his vomit was entirely caviar,
Wednesdays XXXXXX. You couldn't touch him
without getting smeared with money.
Between everything and nothingness:
a pair of mink handcuffs. The hour passed
while he dried under the wing beats
of gnats and televisions
tense as the interval between hiccups
then normal service resumed. Appreciating.

Lives of the Noncombatants

Poor Lorca, all those butterflies
in his bulletholes and there's only
one lousy stranger to throw dirt on him.
When the Falange threatened to set fire
to his home, the stranger volunteered
to save his children, each shovelful
doesn't fall on a daughter, each clod bouncing
in an open eye unearths a son.
There's a song that can't be translated.
The stars in it make no sense
but are very bright. We knock
at the window, we knock at the wind.
God shoots up her hand then pulls it back,
the question's not what she thought
was being asked. We knock at the door,
the ceiling, the floor, the century.

Poor Lorca, what a sissy, his whole life
he knew this was coming and still
he looks like an idiot, suddenly
he stops defanging the piano in his underwear
and gets all morbid, embarrassing the diplomats.
He asks his parents for more money
for a silver pant leg, wristwatches
to fill a fishbowl and then he turns around
and puts tar in his hair. His stage directions
call for a rain of stiff white gloves.
You know what it's like to be wakened
by dogs, don't you? What it's like

to drop a couple thousand feet?
You know what a shovel is, don't you?
The only way we can withstand his berries
is by boiling them in an iron pot
then straining the mush through a cloth
and throwing away what comes through
and throwing away what's left then
wrapping the cloth around our heads
and even then our dreams will almost kill us.

I See a Lily on Thy Brow

It is 1816 and you gash your hand unloading
a crate of geese, but if you keep working
you'll be able to buy a bucket of beer
with your potatoes. You're probably 14 although

no one knows for sure and the whore you sometimes
sleep with could be your younger sister
and when your hand throbs to twice its size
turning the fingernails green, she knots

a poultice of mustard and turkey grease
but the next morning, you wake to a yellow
world and stumble through the London streets
until your head implodes like a suffocated

fire stuffing your nose with rancid smoke.
Somehow you're removed to Guy's Infirmary.
It's Tuesday. The surgeon will demonstrate
on Wednesday and you're the demonstration.

Five guzzles of brandy then they hoist you
into the theater, into the trapped drone
and humid scuffle, the throng of students
a single body staked with a thousand peering

bulbs and the doctor begins to saw. Of course
you'll die in a week, suppurating on a camphor-
soaked sheet but now you scream and scream,
plash in a red river, in sulfuric steam

but above you, the assistant holding you down,
trying to fix you with sad, electric eyes
is John Keats.

Lives of the Dead

So I left my kingdom. Granted
by most standards, it wasn't much of a kingdom:
a glacier up north, a few butterflies, a moat.
It's the moat I miss most, how it made me feel
I could wake up screaming about the Big Hand
and immediately be calmed by its murmur,
my moat out there breathing, never catching fire,
never doing battle with the dominant paradigm,
never rhyming or messing with the syntax, not dying
of some disease where its joints swell up, not
making videos of cutting itself with razor blades,
not calling from the jail all tranquilized,
not deserting me, not saying You owe me,
no smoked windows, no ridicule, no getting
or spending, just taking care of a few frogs
and being somewhat unnavigable like love.
But one day you look up into the sarcophagus
of dust in the rafters and realize you're not
getting any younger. There is indeed a primeval
structure ordained to our lives but it gets
awfully kinked up in its box so I left, I took
my oboe on the road where I was no one, just another
oboist bereft of an orchestra. Never had I been
so sad and exhilarated among the wanton commoners
and their moan became my own but that's when
I came upon my father alone in the garden,
in rags, hair ostinatoed with crows.
Inside my chest was a helicopter against which
traditional forms of nomenclature flailed.

Father, I beseeched, but he was having trouble
with his landing gear. Let the chambermaids
hang themselves, he yelled. It was a public afternoon
but a private midnight, twitch grass amok,
no moon. I tried to think of a scar
we could know each other by but he was Rimbauded
in a world all his own, saluted by phantom under-staff.
Sparks fell into puddles and hissed
and threw their arms out and cursed,
kissed each other and wrote big checks.
Father, I've come back, I cry
not knowing where I am.

Sleep Cycle

We cannot push ourselves away
from this quiet, even in our sprees
of inattention, the departing passengers
stubbing out their smokes, arrivees in tears,
lots of cellophane, the rumpus over parking.

Wind scrapes leaves across the road,
first flashes of snow, it is dark then
it's really dark. Forgive me for not
writing for so long, I've been
right beside you, one of the vaguer
divinities blocking your way with its need
to confess all its botched attempts at love,
what started the whole mess. I love this place,
its absurd use of balustrade, the chairs
that dig into the spine, motorcyclists
propping their drunk girlfriends in the sun,
men playing timed chess with themselves,
the guarantees and warnings that entice us
to the brink of what they warn about.

But we can do no more than pass through
these rooms and their sudden chills
where once a plea was entered almost
unintentionally that seemed at last
to reveal ourselves to ourselves,
immaculate, bereft, deserving to be found.

Troy, Indiana

Under the asphalt: brick and under the brick: clay.
Under the clay: limestone, under the limestone:
volcanic pressure and the well-oiled, first baseman's mitt of
  Bill Nelson
that I lost.

How will future generations know
under the deep-fleeced tree is the body of my cat
but if they have cans and can open them,
he will ectoplasmicly appear,
his mew urgent but un-angsted.

Maybe their sensitive, futuristic equipment
will reveal why he couldn't stand
the mulberry-eyed girlfriend of Bill Nelson.

Perhaps it was her owls.

I was never where I promised to be but
the rosy-fingered girlfriend of Bill Nelson found me
or at least the pottery shards.

The score was 7 to 3 in the midst of a comeback.

This rock I carried from my island nation to place here
where the strong-greaved girlfriend of Bill Nelson
gave me a cape-clasp and a swiss army knife,

the big one with the shrimp deveiner,
and future generations won't have a clue.

They'll think we just sat around
turning to dust, eating preservatives,
blaming us that their atmosphere no longer blocks
the oath-shouting gamma rays

so they won't know what it was like
to lie under the fast-shipped sun
reading a Russian novel
beside the far-shadowing girlfriend of Bill Nelson

for more than 2 seconds otherwise they'd fry
which misses the point of the Russian novel.

I must admit I too was missing the point of the Russian novel
lying beside the wheat-smelling breast-shining girlfriend of Bill
    Nelson
and her spray bottle.
Wolves raced the carriage across the steppes.
A monkey said the flute was full of fire.
Fetal robots trolled the river.
I shot the sheriff but I did not shoot the deputy.

Farewell, Bill Nelson. I'll kill the houseplants
you leave me when you leave first.

Farewell snooty natural food store
where the winged-brain girlfriend of Bill Nelson
worked for a 15% discount and 20% moral superiority.

Kiss kiss, angelic lick lick. Rough rough. Tick tick.
The condom ripped over the harp.
Orpheus never had to put up with this shit.
The condom ripped over the vodka.
A baby fox is a kit. Good fever, good fit.
Wolves raced the carriage across the steppes.

Farewell house where I'd sleep on the ceiling
but keep falling off even though I was ionized
from passing between the anode and cathode
of Bill Nelson and the sharp-shinned girlfriend of Bill Nelson
like a polyester bowling shirt tossed all night
among cotton undies.

I was limping all the time.
My aim was hopeless.
I paid for the abortion
and still no one would accept the terms of my surrender.

One hundred days the quarry where we skinny-dipped
boiled with arms and legs and blades and breasts
and eyes and yeses and gears. Oh, said

the many-willed girlfriend of Bill Nelson
which I took to be the beginning of okay
so I pushed in further.

Future generations!
How I hate you for being alive and unburied
while I am not
but Oh she said and deeper I pushed deeper.

And You Don't Even Have to Leave the Building

But you will have to be rescued by shadows.
The fundamental principles of comedy and
tragedy differ only in the last act.
The appearance of peacocks may suggest
festivity but, when you get right down to it,

they're nasty and unclean, and if you've ever
tried to toss them crumbs, you know exactly
what I mean. To be wounded by a peacock:
tragic or comic? But enough about you.
When I was born, I stank. There was a feeling

not unlike burning. I have worked as yeoman
flogger, igniter of rags, figment in the stop-
gap appeasements a long, long way from home.
My mother I never knew and here is my plea to you.
Our brothers, poorly provisioned in the prickly

outreaches, bicker among staggering mules.
Our sisters run dry of ores, gears freeze.
Preventable, all of it preventable.
Twenty dollars buys so little yet
so much twine! To discover a leak

in a bicycle tire, plunge the tube
into a bucket of water and squeeze, prompting
the diagnostic bubbles. Alas, the same thing
cannot be done with the human heart. Subsiding
is the summer morn and ne'er oft the welkin . . .

well, it is difficult to go on. Please, how
can too much be asked? Yes, I *was* educated
in Bath but through no fault of my own,
the forms were incendiary. For a short while
was a member of the Blue Urger group but refusal

to sketch harbors in fog with eyes unclosed
led to expulsion, wandering, and arrest yet
I love harbors in fog. My skin was not always
thus. Mental lapses, sure, who don't?
Renounced all past work. Painted Tug in '87.

Refused to sign Document of Reformed Depicters,
accused of unearthly sympathies by counterresistance,
of mud-wallowing by intransigent hangers-on.
Renounced all past work. Same old same old.
J, mostly in red, a series, never completed,

I loved her so. Helped to the stage, hat
kept blowing off. Seashells, menacing
seashells impossible to ignore. Recognize
no one. Am survived unmarked in Pennsylvania.

Action Figuring

Maybe this is a guy thing but I find
pizza almost completely sustaining.
One does not have meals, one has pizza
and thus is able to work unimpeded
upon one's theories. One gunman,
definitely one gunman. Such simplicity,
however, can lead to murderous boredom.
In the last 3 days, I have rented 8 videos,
have seen explode: helicopters, satellites,
a bridge, flesh-eating puppets, heads,
hands, the White House, unclassifiable
weaponry, flora and fauna of distant worlds
and still within me some fuse burns on.
Love is not everything yet without it
one explosion is much like any other.
Monday, mine own true saboteur returns
to complicate my diet and napping
deliciously although there will be infinitely
more dishes, more fuzz. Sex isn't
everything but inside each of us is
a sort of timer, a sort of spring.
My one and only detonator comes with
many small accessories which, if she was
an army man, would be: grenades, bazookas,
flame-throwers, all in danger of being
sucked up a vacuum cleaner hose. I believe
everyone should have the opportunity
to sift through dust and hair and find
an emerald. On the whole, I am in favor

of the sense that "things are more complicated
than one at first thought" which makes one
nervous often in a good, young-in-
the-fingertips way. You could be washing
your car, you could be gleaning naught
from the printed media while inside
is this flying then, gee, how did all
this fruit salad get here? But wait!
Can we ever be sure it is fruit salad
and not some sort of bomb? One gazes into
the other's eyes and sees the reflection
of one's regrettable nose but more importantly
a darkness that is seeing depth itself
unless one uses ophthalmological equipment
and then examines the retina and vascularization
and vitreous humor which in composition
is very akin to amniotic fluid. I can't remember
swimming without remembering almost drowning.
Either one is about to be frightened to death
or this is prelude to a kiss.

My Fall Teaching Schedule

We were trying to unload the Pope.
Breton says we've got to open a trapdoor
in the sky but he also says shoot randomly
into the crowd. In the act of dying,

even Pascal clung to a delusive fallacy.
A lot of guys think we should use
the sand trick that worked for the pyramids
but that'd make us too expendable. Sure'd

be easier if we could work piece by piece
but because this is the Infallible,
you gotta unload the whole sucker at once.
Is man composed solely of yearning?

Nope, there's a lot of cinder in there.
Under the direction of Bernardo Rosselino,
the civic, democratic and ecclesiastic
building of Pienza took shape between

1459 and 1464, but his Pope was a feather
compared to ours. His Pope wore burlap
underwear that afforded a more robust grip
but those were different times, even

a cornfield could become possessed
and a lot of school kids had to be burned.
But this Pope, there's no mercy in him,
just a very pointy surface over silken

briefs. Some of the leftist-leaning guys
think we should let him slip, dent the eminence.
What is it called when the soul smells like
a black walnut and is just as hard to get at?

Can you kill someone with a poisoned glove?
Is Being a river or is it a shock? What
a useless Pope, just one big chunk of glitter.
A whole lifetime of eating god's body and

he still can't say how it tastes.

Even Funnier Looking Now

If someone had asked me then,
Do you suffer from the umbrage of dawn's
dark race horses, is your heart a prisoner
of raindrops? Hell yes! I would have said
or No way! Never would I have said,
What could you possibly be talking about?
I had just gotten to the twentieth century
like a leftover girder from the Eiffel Tower.
My Indian name was Pressure-Per-Square-Inch.
I knew I was made of glass but I didn't
yet know what glass was made of: hot sand
inside me like pee going all the wrong
directions, probably into my heart
which I knew was made of gold foil
glued to dust. It was you I loved,
only you but you kept changing
into different people which made
kissing your mouth very exciting.
Of the birds, I loved the crows best,
sitting in their lawn chairs, ranting
about their past campaigns, the broken
supply lines, the traitors. Some had bodies
completely covered with feathers like me,
some were almost invisible like you.
And of the rivers, I loved the Susquehanna,
how each spring it would bring home a boy
who didn't listen disguised as a sack of mud.
Everyone knew if you were strong enough
and swam fast and deep enough, you'd reach

another city but no one was ever strong enough.
Along the banks: the visceral honeysuckle.
That was the summer we tanned on the roof
reading the Russians. You told me
you broke up with your boyfriend I lost count.
Dusky, pellucid and grave.
In the Chekhov story, nothing happened but
a new form of misery was nonetheless delineated.
Accidentally, I first touched your breast.
Rowboat, I tried to think of rhymes for rowboat.
And sequins and yellow and two-by-fours.
In one of your parents' bathrooms,
the handles were silver dolphins.
My ears were purple.
The crayons melted in the sun,
that was one way. Another was to tear things up
and tape them together wrong.
That was the summer I lived in the attic
and the punk band never practiced below.
Your breasts were meteors, never meteorites.
There was something wrong with my tongue.
There was my famous use of humor
that Jordan said was the avoidance of emotion.
I couldn't hold on to a nickel.
There was that pitcher on the mound,
older, facing his former team. He had lost
some of his stuff but made up for it with
cerebrum. Your breasts were never rusty.
Your breasts reflected the seeming-so.
Your mouth I wanted my mouth over,
your eyes my eyes into,

into your Monday afternoons I would try to cram
my Sunday nights, into your anthropology paper
I wanted to put my theories,
your apartment I would put my records in
and never get them back.
Here, you said: another baby avocado tree.
You threw your shoe. I broke
the refrigerator and the fossil fish.
I broke my shoulder blade.
I tried to make jambalaya.
To relax the organism, the cookbook said,
pound with a mallet on the head or shell.
Your friends all thought you were crazy.
My friends all thought I was crazy.
The names of Aztec gods were on one page,
serotonin uptake inhibitors on the other.
You fell in the street carrying a pumpkin.
I walked home alone in the snow.
I broke my hand.
Your light meter was in my glove box.

A Poem by Dean Young

Don't think for one fucking instant
that I don't have a broken heart.
The man in briefs in an infinite sea
believes there is no subconscious
nor is he aware that tempora exists.
Don't think I have not eaten
in the most beautiful Chinese restaurant
in the world. Don't think I have not written
on the walls of my bathtub.
Don't think I haven't poisoned a snail.
Don't think I haven't ignited
the sulfur of the fortune teller.
Of course I have written a poem by Dean Young!
More than once I have written a poem by Dean Young.
More than once I have left them by your gate.
More than once I have stuffed the eucalyptus leaves
in your mouth. More than once I have lived,
more than once I have died because of it.
I love you. This remarkable statement
has appeared on earth to substantiate the clams.
Perhaps now we can reach an agreement in the Himalayas,
returning shortly thereafter as gods, the kind kind
largely ignored by larger and more sensitive organisms.
Don't think I wasn't shocked when
you were a traffic signal
and I a woodpecker.

I Can Hardly Be Considered
a Reliable Witness

First there was a raffle conducted by silhouettes
then some gaga clangor and the deflection
of not getting what I wanted probably never.
I was trying to write The Indomitability
of the Human Spirit to impress you but
it kept coming out The Undomesticated
Human Spigot, a blowhard stoned soap opera.
I couldn't understand anything and you
were my teacher. The rain bounced off
the upturned canoes by the man-made lake
and out of the man-made water small bodies
propelled themselves into the nevertheless air.

This I could not do.

I had been worn out by a lasagna.
A train had run through my almanac.
I had gone directly to the small screen.
It was only a couple times I leaned from the window
in that gorilla mask yet of all I have accomplished
and delayed, my deeds in the outback, cradling
the dying wombats, cataloging every wrong
ever done to me with innovative
cross-references, this is what I'm remembered for:
leaning from a window in a gorilla mask.

It's frustrating,
like hiding stolen jewelry in tubs of lard.
Sure, it works but have you ever tried
to get grease off a brooch?
Or geese out of a coach for that matter.
They have to be heavily sedated
and it's weeks before they can even float right.

Not in Any Ha Ha Way

I went to the grocery store
and pressed my ear against the butter
and it cried out and I pressed my ear
against the paper towels and they cried out
but of what I cannot tell. All was
as one jellied equation that ended
with the symbol for oblivion although
it could have been a mistake,
something half-erased. Obviously,
there was no question about going down
the catfood lightbulb hygiene aisle.
We had been warned maybe a thousand times
to enjoy ourselves but outside, the sky
had turned fustian and doggy, there was
rain then sunshine making the executives
with umbrellas go from looking like geniuses
to prim morons. Oh how I wanted my lips
pressed against your parachute jacket but
you were wearing your cloak of not-being-there.
Is all that a culture can hope to produce
interesting ruins for the absent gods
to sweep their metal detectors through?
Surely, I am not the one to ask.
There is a sidereal embezzlement to my days
made indescribable with eclipses, car payments,
wounded sofas, parts of the rose bush
fifteen feet long, approximately the length
of childhood. You are not the first
to ask me to describe this darkness,

it is the job I've never wanted but
am always overqualified for, being
too zealous and confused just as scientists,
after introducing electrodes into the monkeys'
diencephalons, still don't know if life
is suffering therefore beautiful or
life is beautiful therefore we must suffer.

Cotton in a Pill Bottle

I love the fog. It's not one hundred degrees.
It's not Mary sobbing on the phone or powder-
white mildew killing the rose. My father
lost inside it keeps pretending he's dead
just so he can get a little peace.
It's not made of fire or afraid of fire
like me, it has nothing to do with smoke.
There's never any ash, anything to sift through.
You just put your hand on the yellow rail
and the steps seem to move themselves.
It doesn't have a job to do.
It's morning all afternoon.
It loves the music but would be
just as happy listening to the game.
Still, I don't know what frightens me.
It doesn't blame anyone.
You'll never see tears on its cheeks.
It'll never put up a fight.
I love how the fog lies down in the air,
how it can get only so far from the sea.

Eidos

Mary suddenly laughs. Of course not yes
no never in a million years. Mary talking
talking. Mary up a tree smoking. Mexican food
with Mary. Quantum mechanics. Everything
flattened, pleated, flush. Inexpensive
metal shelving full of doll parts.
Typical of such work, a grid of interlocking
rectangles is juxtaposed with a pile of rubble.
How hard it is to get at the human heart.
Mary talking about falconry, about hail.
At any moment an announcement's expected
but that's what moments are for, always
something destroyed, something raised
from the ocean floor and subsequent legal
wrangles. She wants to wrap the trees in silk.
Next slide. Identical blocks of creosote
may mean the body is a bird in flight
stilled by electroshock. Typical of such work,
the blood is fake but the bleeding's real.
Getting at her heart. Getting her to shut up
about Agnes Martin and polar exploration.
Mary suddenly in tears. Actually it's fiberglass.
Eidos means, in Greek, a visceral image
of a mental state. There's no such thing
as a mistake. Does she ever sleep? As if
by accident: a delicate feather, the face
rubbed out, the face replaced by a bunch of grapes.
When the maggots pupate, the show's over.
Hot water in a rock declivity. Mary suddenly

alone, her boat capsized, never seen again.
Alternately, moves to Berlin, starts an influential
magazine. Wood crutches, bathrobes, newspaper,
glue, bone. Dimensions unknown.

Pulse

This time, the illusion took the shape
of a house I lived in for nine years.
What polish! Rooms oscillating with light,
a rose thorn casting a thorn shadow,

grays twinged with blues. What fine detail.
Forsythia, salt, eight-foot extension cords.
You could walk into a door and your head
would think it was bleeding. Sometimes

the dead people would let their children
play in the street with their remote control
monster trucks. Even if you scratched a surface
to blister, under it would be another surface

like a drawing of a bowl of peaches under
a painting of a pile of skulls. And the dirt!
Look at it under a microscope, you'd see
encyclopedias, ganglions, arks, huge gears,

Dürer at work with his grids.
A hawk tore apart a dove in the backyard.
You could smell lightning smelt the air
so who could blame me for how far I slipped

into belief? Pick a card, any card,
it'd never be blank. My wife, even asleep,
didn't turn to dust and when I was dying,
I was given milligrams of chemicals

as if my belief could not be mocked
and I thought I was healed
as if my belief could not be mocked.
Every spill traversed its singular stain

and no matter how quickly I turned around,
I'd never catch any of it dissolving.
But a few times, lying in the dark
that was never really dark, I thought

I saw a cup or book or handkerchief
pulse like a thing about to fall apart.

What a Good Horse I Have

What a good horse I have.
He lets me walk beside him humming
because I never learned the words.
He finds my nightmares banal,

even the one with the big father-head
saying No in the desert. My mother
thinks candy bars cost one hundred dollars,
my hometown looks like a damsel fly

drowned in ink, a mechanic keeps
slapping my sister, my government's
dropping bombs again, beaches dotted
with syringes but what a good horse.

It doesn't bother him that no one
meets you after death, not a brother
or underling immune to the pathos
of a joke. When I get drunk

and want to piss all over the firmament,
he doesn't flinch from our task.
Which is what? I scream,
throwing down my bloody gloves,

breaking my sunglasses over my knee
but he never answers which is how
he keeps me going
past the grinning marquees,

through the simmer of orange groves,
past the schoolhouses where
children are eating paint.

Archon

Something set it off,
a burst of light or
new contaminant in the soil
and I can go no further
pretending
these things do not affect me
personally
as a wren is affected
by a slant of afternoon
and flies off to other continents.
You I could not leave.
Your tears were not
what I needed
yet you gave them,
thin silky fluid
unsuitable for the longevity
they wished to represent.
The longevity of suffering, I suppose.
Somehow, that night,
we got you into your gown.
Your father made an appearance,
giving directions
only you could hear,
dirt clinging to his lapels.
Soon we'd lay you
in the field behind the mansion
where as a child
you'd watch for hawks.
I don't know

what you thought
the world was for.
Nymph grasshoppers
triggering
the strawberry plants,
voices seeking you out,
as calm a place as any
to be shattered,
not far
from the river,
sky without a mark,
shadow knitted to the ground.

Noncompliant

I was born in Pennsylvania before
the plain folk discovered amyl nitrate
and elected a stripper regent.
We had two pleasures: swimming in clouds
which we called prayer and going to the fridge
in the sweaty night and pausing there
in the cold exhale of light
before being torn away
and that was the sermon.
I wasn't put on this earth to explain.
In those days, you'd spend a week weaving
yourself a straw hat
God would smite in an instant
over some commandment technicality
so you were never alone, even masturbating.
So we sat around drinking tea
that tasted like flying ants
trying to decide what happens after death.
Of course everything sounded like
another version of life:
the blazing filament, constant ice cream,
Big Eagle tearing you apart then regurgitating
you for its chicks, obscure statutes regarding
oral sex, you'd get everything you ever
wanted because you wouldn't want it anymore.
Before opening the door, be sure it isn't hot
in case where you're going is in flames.
Sunlight falls upon the stone stairs.
I loved my friends and they helped me

with the electrodes in my pjs.

Somehow I endured.

Sure you did, says the wind locked on the exercycle.

The roses in riot over the fence.

The dream life measured out in fluid ounces.

Maybe next time, says the wave upon the tarry beach.

What next time? says the moon.

It hardly has to do with my heart

although that's the preponderance of gathered data.

Starlight falls upon the stone stairs.

The river is a river of mist.

Not the gulp, the sip.

Great flocks of machinery muster on near hills.

How I Get My Ideas

Sometimes you just have to wait
15 seconds then beat the prevailing nuance
from the air. If that doesn't work,
try to remember how many times
you've wakened in the body of an animal,
two arms, two legs, willowy antennae.
Try thinking what it would be like
to never see your dearest again.
Stroke her gloves, sniff his overcoat.
If that's a no-go, call Joe
who's never home but keeps changing
the melody of his message.
Cactus at night emits its own light,
the river flows under the sea.
Dear face I always recognize but never
know, everything has a purpose
from which it must be freed,
maybe with crowbars, maybe the gentlest breeze.
Always turn in the direction of the skid.
If it's raining, use the rain
to lash the windowpanes or,
in a calmer mode, deepen the new greens
nearly to a violet. I can't live
without violet although it's red
I most often resort to.
Sometimes people become angelic when they cry,
sometimes only ravaged.
Technically, Mary still owes me a letter,
her last was just porcupine quills and tears,

tears that left a whitish residue
on black construction paper.
Sometimes I look at used art books at Moe's
just to see women without their clothes.
How can someone so rich,
who can have fish whenever he wants,
go to baseball games,
still feel such desperation?
I'm afraid I must insist
on desperation. By the fourth week
the embryo has nearly turned itself
inside out. If that doesn't help,
you'll just have to wait which
may involve sleeping which may involve
dreaming and sometimes dreaming works.
Father, why have you returned,
dirt on your morning vest?
You cannot control your laughter.
You cannot control your love.
You know not to hit the brakes on ice
but do anyway. You bend the nail
but keep hammering because
hammering makes the world.

Acknowledgements

Some of these poems first appeared in the following magazines (some in earlier versions). Thanks to the editors of *American Letters & Commentary, Bellingham Review, Bug Tussle, Conduit, Crazyhorse, Fence, Forklift, Gettysburg Review, Green Mountains Review, Harvard Review, Jubilat, Kenyon Review, New American Writing, Ohio Review, Ploughshares, Puerto del Sol, Sycamore Review, Threepenny Review, Tri-Quarterly,* and *Volt.*

"Lives of the Mind," and "Lives of the Noncombatants" appeared in *Previous Life,* a chapbook designed by Sharon DeGraw and published by the Center for the Book, Iowa City.

Thanks to David Rivard, Donald Revell, Dobby Gibson, Mary Ruefle, David Wojahn, Keith Ratzlaff, Kevin Stein, Ed Ochester, Matt Hart, Wendy Lesser, Joe DiPrisco, and Jim Galvin.

"Bright Window" is for Brenda Hillman.

"The River Merchant, Stuck in Kalamazoo . . ." owes a debt to James Shea.

"Sources of the Delaware" appeared in *Best American Poetry 2001.*

"A Poem by Dean Young" was written by Mary Ruefle. Its companion, "A Poem by Mary Ruefle" written by Dean Young, may be found among her work.

Impossible soundtrack: David Torn, Gastr del Sol, Thomas Mapfumo, David Sylvian.

Thank you, Kenneth Koch
& my brother, Tony Hoagland.

Dean Young has published four previous books of poems, *First Course in Turbulence* (University of Pittsburgh Press, 1999); *Strike Anywhere* (1995), which won the Colorado Poetry Prize; *Beloved Infidel* (1992); and *Design with X* (1988). His poems have appeared in several editions of *The Best American Poetry* as well as in numerous literary journals. A recipient of the Stegner fellowship from Stanford University and two fellowships from the National Endowment for the Arts, Young is on the faculty of the Warren Wilson M.F.A. program in creative writing and the visiting faculty of the Iowa Writers' Workshop. He lives in Berkeley with wife, the novelist Cornelia Nixon and his cat, Keats.